Y0-DJM-935

THE
KOREAN
WAR

Richard Edwards

ROURKE ENTERPRISES INC.
Vero Beach, Florida 32964

Text © 1988 Rourke Enterprises Inc. *90-17445*
PO Box 3328, Vero Beach, Florida, 32964

Library of Congress Cataloging-in-Publication Data

Edwards, Richard, 1943–
    The Korean War/Richard Edwards.
        p.   cm.—(Flashpoints)
    British ed. published: Hove, East Sussex, England: Wayland, 1987.
    Bibliography: p.
    Includes index.
    Summary: Discusses the origins, events, conclusion, and aftermath
of the conflict in Korea following the Communist invasion of the
southern half of the country.
    ISBN 0-86592-036-2
    1. Korean War, 1950–1953—Juvenile literature.   [1. Korean War,
1950–1953.]   I. Title.   II. Series: Flashpoints (Vero Beach, Fla.)
DS918.E38   1989
951.9'042—dc19
                                                          88-2455
                        55541   CIP
                                                             AC

Manufactured in England

Contents

1
The lost war

On January 12, 1950, the U.S. Secretary of State, Dean Acheson, addressed the National Press Club in Washington D.C. He made the announcement that, in line with the U.S. policy of containing communism within certain geographical boundaries, the defensive perimeter in the Pacific would run from the Aleutians, off Alaska, down to Japan, the Ryukyus Islands and the Philippines. Countries lying beyond this perimeter would have to rely initially upon their own resources to repel any communist advances.

Opposite *The U.S. line of defense in the Pacific was set in 1950 and ran from the Aleutians to the Philippines.*

Right *The invasion of South Korea shocked and surprised the world.*

8

COMMUNISTS INVADE SOUTH KOREA

TANKS 20 MILES FROM CAPITAL: CALL FOR AID

U.S. ARMS REPORTED ON WAY FROM JAPAN

SECURITY COUNCIL CONDEMN ACT OF AGGRESSION

Soviet-dominated North Korea launched an attack at dawn yesterday on the southern half of the country. While troops and tanks crossed the frontier and invasion ships sailed down the east coast, planes attacked the airfield at Seoul, the southern capital.

Within a few hours the Northern army had stormed over the 38th parallel, the border between the two States, and had occupied all the territory north of the Imjin river. South Korea mobilised its troops and sent them by train, lorry, bus and car to meet the invaders.

Early to-day fierce fighting was reported north and north-east of Seoul. The Northern troops crossed the river with 90 tanks and reached a point 20 miles from the capital.

Further east the Southern defenders seized a town five miles north of the 38th parallel. Meanwhile attacks from the sea were reported on the

MR. TRUMAN FLIES BACK TO WASHINGTON

EARLY DECISION ON ARMS AID LIKELY

FROM OUR OWN CORRESPONDENT
WASHINGTON, Sunday.

President Truman to-day cut short his week-end in Independence, Missouri, and flew back to Washington. His decision followed a telephone conversation with Mr. Acheson, Secretary of State, on the situation in Korea

His assistant Press Secretary, Mr. Ayres, said the President was "concerned but not alarmed" by the attack. He would make no other comment.

Mr. Acheson returned to the State Department this afternoon. He immediately had a conference with Mr. Pace, Secretary for the Army; Mr. Webb, Under-Secretary of State; Mr. Rusk and Mr. Hickerson, Assistant Secretaries of State, and Dr. Jessup, Ambassador-at-Large.

"COULD BE DANGEROUS"

Mr. Truman had planned to return to-morrow morning but changed his plan after the telephone conversation. Announcing the decision. Mr. Ayres said: "Mr. Truman has three or four important decisions to make," and felt he should be back in Washington immediately.

Mr. Truman said he would not have anything to say until he knew all the facts. "It could be a dangerous situation, but I hope not. There has been no formal declaration of war—that I know of."

He indicated that on his arrival in Washington he would go immediately to the White House for conferences with Mr. Acheson and Mr. Johnson, Defence Secretary.

One of the "important decisions" responsible for President Truman's change of plans may well have been the question of diverting arms from Gen. MacArthur's command in Japan.

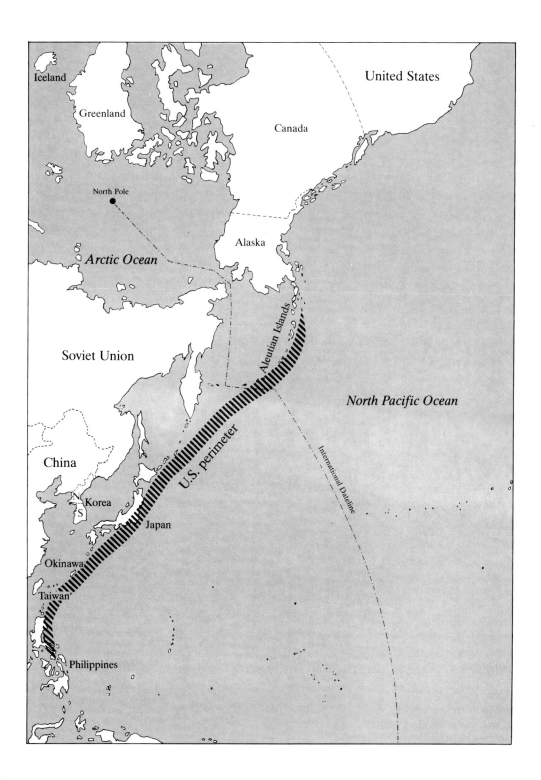

To the Korean people this announcement meant that the fate of their country, temporarily divided at the end of World War II, was to be left to them. In the Republic of Korea (South Korea), the speech was greeted with horror by the government of Syngman Rhee, which feared the superior military might of the communist regime in the Democratic People's Republic of Korea (North Korea). The North Korean government, under Kim Il Sung, believed that the reunification of the country under communist control could be achieved easily without the interference of the United States, and planned its strategy accordingly.

The possibility of North Korean troops being introduced into the South was a constant threat, but its actual occurrence, beginning on June 25, 1950, came as a complete surprise. The Americans were caught unprepared. As the North Korean troops advanced into the South to link up with anti-government forces within the country itself, the U.S. President, Harry S. Truman, met with his advisers to decide what to do. The policy formed a few months earlier was effectively reversed and the United States pledged to provide military support for the crumbling regime of Syngman Rhee in the South.

Thus, on June 26, the Pacific Command was ordered to provide limited military support to the Southern forces, under the leadership of General Douglas MacArthur. Initially, that took the form of a naval blockade and the bombing of positions south of the 38th parallel, the line dividing the country. On June 30, following MacArthur's recommendation, the decision to introduce ground troops was taken as the only way to halt the communist advance. Truman gave the order, and the seeds of three years of increasingly bloody conflict were sown.

The U.S. and U.N. intervene

The first detachment of American troops was airlifted into Korea on July 1 and rushed to the front to counter the communist offensive. A decision was taken to build a defensive line around the southeastern port of Pusan, and during the next few months, troops and materials poured into this area.

To justify its position, the United States had sought and obtained the support of the United Nations for its actions. At the U.N. on June 27, the U.S. Ambassador, Warren Austin, had called for stringent sanctions against North Korea. He

Opposite General Douglas MacArthur in South Korea, three days after the invasion from the North. On his recommendation, U.S. ground troops were introduced to counter the attack.

10

recommended that U.N. member states should provide assistance to South Korea to repel aggression and restore peace. In the absence of the Soviet delegate, who was boycotting the United Nations for its failure to recognize the new communist government in China, the resolution was passed. The dispute over the fate of Korea, initially an issue for Koreans, was therefore swiftly and increasingly internationalized. Support for the U.N. resolution to provide military personnel to back the U.S. forces eventually came from fifteen members, including Britain, France, Canada and Australia. By the end of 1951, overall United Nations

On July 1, the first detachment of U.S. troops was airlifted into Korea. Here, troops are disembarking onto beaches on the east coast of South Korea.

forces numbered in the region of 600,000 personnel, nearly half of whom were American.

On July 7, MacArthur was placed in charge of all U.N. forces, with the remaining South Korean troops also under his command. As the North Korean forces advanced to occupy all but the southeastern corner of the peninsula, the stage was now set for a full-scale conflict, which was to wage back and forth across the country until the eventual stalemate the following year. In the three years the conflict lasted, there was untold destruction and huge casualties. Figures for those killed, wounded, captured or missing

13

British troops in Korea. By the end of 1951 about 600,000 U.N. and U.S. troops were involved in the conflict.

totaled around 995,000 U.S. and U.N. troops. Casualties for North Koreans and the Chinese "volunteers" (who were eventually to come to the aid of the North) are uncertain. Estimates run into the region of 1.5 million. The majority of casualties were civilians who became caught up in the ebb and flow of the war.

The principal tragedy of the Korean War is that the conflict to overcome the temporary division of Korea had, in the end, resulted in the country's becoming even more deeply divided. Although reunification remains a contentious issue in Korea to this day, it is an issue and a war that has largely been forgotten by the rest of the world. Supplanted in the public mind by the televised war in Vietnam, the importance and significance of the Korean War has been lost. It was in Korea that Communist China first entered the world stage as a major power. The Korean war is also an important example of the post World War II trend for the fate of countries to be determined by the strategic interests of the major powers, rather than by the people of those countries themselves. The intervention of the United States and other United Nations member countries provided the springboard for an extension of the conflict beyond the immediate concerns of the Korean people. Their fate and the fate of their country became increasingly dependent upon the support, interests and policies of the major world powers, particularly the United States, the Soviet Union and China.

This signboard marks the dividing line between North and South Korea.

2
An occupied nation

Korea has a long tradition of national unity and stability. For 500 years, from 1392, it was ruled by the Yi dynasty as an independent country paying tribute to its more powerful neighbor, China. For many years Korea, having suffered periods of occupation and attempts at intervention in its affairs by China and Japan, effectively cut itself off from the outside world. It was only in the nineteenth century that this position changed.

At that time, Japan was itself emerging from a long period of isolation and seeking to spread its influence in Northeast Asia. Japan was undergoing a process of industrialization and needed markets and raw materials to supplement its own resources. It was looking to increase its territorial control in the region, and Korea, its near neighbor, was an obvious target. In 1876, Japan managed to obtain a trade treaty with the reluctant Koreans and this was the start of increasing Japanese penetration into the internal affairs of the country, which was eventually to lead to its annexation in 1910.

Becoming a Japanese colony gave rise to different reactions among the Korean people. Some welcomed the Japanese, feeling that the industrialization and efficiency they brought with them was more progressive than the stagnant rule of the Yi dynasty. However, the increasing control over the economic, social and political life of the country by the Japanese also engendered wide-scale resentment and resistance. Opposition to its colonial status began to increase and take more organized forms.

Opposite *For many years, the Japanese held control in Korea. This formal portrait shows a young Korean prince with his Japanese tutor.*

Struggle for independence
In March 1919, the Koreans began a nationwide nonviolent protest at Japanese rule. A proclamation of independence was signed by Korean political leaders. However, this

16

In 1919, Korea signed a declaration of independence and began its struggle to break free from Japanese domination. It did not do so until the Japanese defeat in World War II. Here, crowds in Pusan, South Korea, celebrate Independence Day in 1950.

passive resistance was met with force by the Japanese. Thousands of demonstrators were killed, while many more were imprisoned and tortured. At that stage, many nationalists fled into exile in other countries, thereby creating rival pockets of opposition to the Japanese, a situation that was to lead to competition to determine the fate of the country during the war.

Three basic centers for opposition to Japan's occupation emerged in China, the United States and the Soviet Union. Nationalists in China and the United States cooperated to form a provisional government in exile under the leadership of the anti-Japanese resistance leader Syngman Rhee. The Koreans based in the Soviet Union initially sought to cooperate with the other nationalist groups. On being rejected because of their commitment to communism, this group developed its own strategy for ousting the Japanese from Korea.

While Syngman Rhee looked to the United States for support in exerting pressure on the Japanese, the communists began to organize the opposition groups within Korea, and in 1935 began a guerrilla war against Japan. Among these guerrillas was Kim Il Sung, who went into exile in the Soviet Union in the late 1930s to fight with the Red Army against Germany in World War II. He was to return to Korea with Soviet troops in 1945, to become head of the North Korean regime and leader of the Korean National Democratic Front.

World War II provided the catalyst for the removal of Japanese forces from Korea. In seeking to extend its empire, Japan allied itself with Germany. With the decision of the Western Allies in 1941 to make the defeat of Hitler in Europe their prime concern, Japan faced only limited resistance in extending its control over much of Asia. Indigenous opposition was of major importance in resisting the spread of Japanese influence, most notably from the Chinese communist forces of Mao Zedong and the nationalist forces of Chiang Kai-Shek.

Enter the Allies

Korea was only of very minor importance to the Western Allies. Roosevelt, Churchill and Stalin agreed that upon the eventual defeat of Japan, Korea should become free and independent "in due course." That angered many Korean nationalists who wished for independence as soon as the

Opposite A British newspaper cartoon published at the end of World War II clearly emphasizes the power and responsibility that now lay in the hands of the victorious Allies.

20

"—And now let's learn to *live* together!"

Kim Il Sung spent several years in exile in the Soviet Union before returning to his country in 1945 to become head of the North Korean regime.

Japanese were defeated. That defeat looked increasingly likely from 1943, especially after Stalin agreed that the Soviet Union would join the war against Japan once victory over Germany had been secured.

The Allies were working in unison for the defeat of the Axis powers (the alliance of Nazi Germany, Fascist Italy and Japan). However, as World War II drew to a close, the underlying rivalry among the Allies for influencing world events began to surface, a rivalry that was to scar the history of Korea.

3
Division and conflict

The Japanese surrendered on August 14, 1945, following the dropping of atomic bombs on the cities of Hiroshima and Nagasaki. The immediate problem confronting the Allies was to disarm the Japanese troops and reestablish some form of government in the territories previously occupied by the Japanese.

The United States found itself with no clear policy for the immediate situation in Korea. It was felt that if independence were granted right away, the communists would become the dominant force in the country. A vague policy of trusteeship had been developed toward the end of the war. According to that policy, the United States would oversee the reestablishment of government in Korea, giving non-communist nationalists a chance to build up their power base among the people. That was felt to be of even greater

On the day of the Japanese surrender, President Truman issued General Order No. 1, which divided Korea at the 38th parallel.

importance following the occupation of Korea by Soviet forces, who were supported by Korean communists, in early August.

On August 14, 1945, President Truman (Roosevelt's successor) approved General Order No. 1, which temporarily divided Korea at the 38th parallel. American troops were to disarm the Japanese forces south of the parallel, and communist troops were to do the same north of the line. The Soviet Union agreed to that, although many Koreans were in opposition.

Between the surrender of the Japanese and the deployment of American troops in Korea from September 8, the Koreans themselves were very active. Opposition groups

This map shows the division of Korea at the 38th parallel.

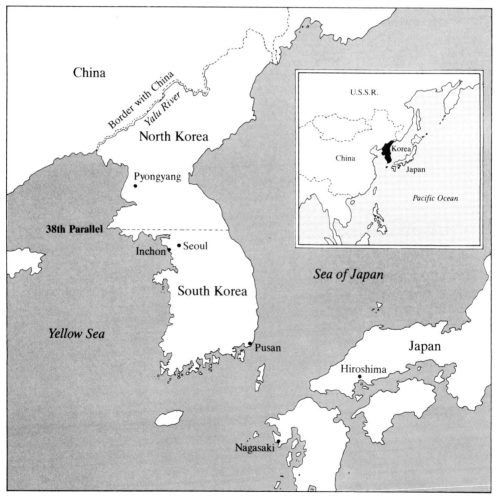

북조선로동당중앙본부

throughout the country established a network of People's Committees set up to disarm the Japanese. These Committees were designed to provide the basis for a nationwide system of government in a newly independent Korea. Although the communists were widely represented in these Committees, they also reflected a broad spectrum of Korean nationalist opinion.

Carrying huge portraits of Stalin and Kim Il Sung, these North Korean communists welcome a joint U.S.–Soviet visiting commission.

Anticommunist Koreans marching in Tokyo, Japan, in protest against the so-called Soviet puppet government established in North Korea.

North of the 38th parallel, Kim Il Sung was installed with Soviet backing as head of a temporary government. Using the People's Committees to administer the North, the communists began to consolidate their influence. The division of the country had cut off the industrialized North from its traditional source of food supplies in the agricultural South. Land reforms were therefore enacted by the government to try to increase food production.

At the time of their arrival in South Korea, the U.S. authorities, unsure of the actual situation within Korea, ignored the representatives of the People's Committees. Initially, they reinstalled Koreans who had collaborated with the Japanese into positions of power to administer the South. That caused large-scale disenchantment, which was to alienate many nationalists from future U.S.-supported regimes. Determined to ensure a noncommunist government, the Americans returned Syngman Rhee from exile in October 1945 to head the Southern administration. To many Koreans who had opposed Japan from within Korea,

農民食堂
大同館茶征合安合員合
電話 二四八二番

Syngman Rhee was an unacceptable leader. There began a spiral of violence in the South, which was to continue through to the outbreak of the war in 1950.

The violence emanated from three major sources. First, it came from the supporters of Rhee, who objected to the division of the country, albeit temporary. They demonstrated in support of immediate U.S. action to remove the

Armed members of the North Korean Constabulary on patrol in the streets of Pyongyang, the Northern capital.

Soviet and communist forces from the North and against American troop withdrawal. Second, violence came from the opponents of Rhee who objected to the suppression of the People's Committees and the increasingly repressive nature of the government. They demonstrated for national reunification to be determined by Koreans alone. The third source of violence was the methods employed by the members of the Korean Constabulary, most of whom had served in similar roles under the Japanese. The Constabulary was used by the Rhee government to quell opposition and suppress uprisings.

North versus South

The temporary division of the country therefore became more entrenched, as the ideologically opposed governments of North and South Korea consolidated their respective holds on political power. If the country had been left to itself, the communists would undoubtedly have played the leading role in creating an independent, unified Korea. The regime in the South, however, found that unacceptable and kept up pressure on the Americans to maintain their presence. That was to lead many Koreans to perceive Rhee as a puppet of the Americans.

The situation was very difficult for American policymakers. Without military support for Rhee, Korea would become communist. However, continued military aid was unrealistic. World War II had only just ended and the United States was loath to enter further conflict. In 1947, the problem was brought before the newly established United Nations.

At the U.N., the United States called for nationwide elections to be held in Korea, followed by the withdrawal of all foreign troops. The Soviet Union proposed withdrawal first and elections to follow. While the U.S. line was supported by Rhee, many opposition groups in the South, as well as the Northern government, supported the Soviet proposal. However, the Western European governments were reliant on American aid for economic reconstruction, and the U.N. voted for the U.S. option. That was rejected by the North Koreans. Separate elections were therefore organized in South Korea, but were opposed by many groups there who felt it reinforced the division of the country.

The election in South Korea took place on May 10, 1948. Rhee and his supporters took the majority of the votes. In a

Opposite *South Koreans casting votes in the first democratic elections held in the country in May 1948.*

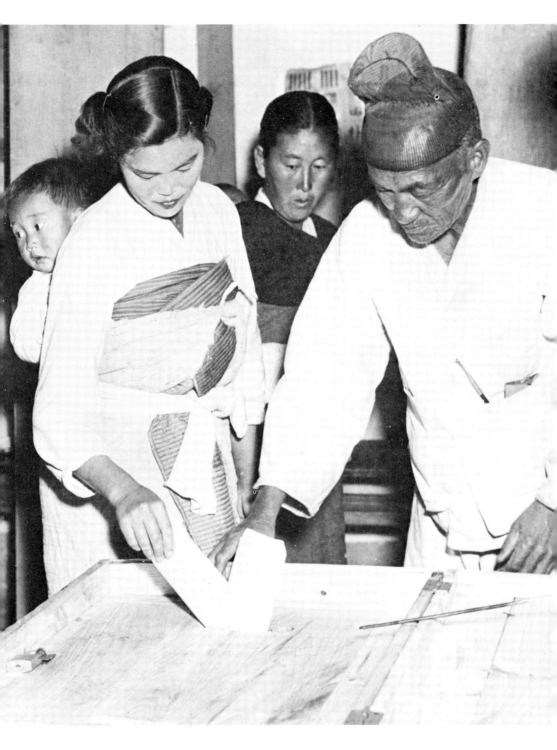

*On August 15, 1948,
Syngman Rhee
became president of
the Republic of
Korea. He is seen
here with General
MacArthur during
ceremonies to mark
the formation of the
new republic.*

situation of increasing internal turmoil, he declared the formation of the Republic of Korea on August 15, 1948, with himself as president. In response, Kim Il Sung announced the formation of the Democratic People's Republic of Korea in the North to coincide with the withdrawal of Soviet troops. The temporary division of the country was looking increasingly permanent. With the withdrawal of American troops by mid-1949, the stage was set for the events of the following year.

In the North, Kim Il Sung had consolidated the communist control of the government, initiated reforms and built up a large Soviet trained and armed Korean People's Army. In

the South, Rhee possessed a weak army and faced growing internal opposition. Large parts of the Republic were in a continual state of unrest, with communist guerrillas giving support to other opposition groups. Armed clashes were a permanent feature along the 38th parallel. When, on June 25, 1950, North Korean troops entered the South, the conflict surrounding the initial division of the country moved into a new phase. What was not anticipated was the scale the conflict would reach.

Soldiers standing guard over communist rebels captured in South Korea during uprisings against the new government.

31

4
Civil war or invasion?

There has been much speculation about the role of the Soviet leader, Joseph Stalin, and the Chinese leader, Mao Zedong, in instigating the conflict in Korea. The reliance of Kim Il Sung's regime upon Soviet aid makes it extremely unlikely that the invasion could have taken place without the support of Stalin. However, to see the war as simply the result of Soviet communist expansionism does little justice to the genuine grievances of the Korean people at the division of their country. In the North, it was the Americans who were

Opposite *These families of captured antigovernment guerrillas were taken from their villages and put under guard.*

Right *The Soviet leader, Joseph Stalin, in 1950. Soviet aid and support encouraged the communist invasion of South Korea.*

90-17445

55541

held responsible for that situation, because it was the Americans who had initially put forward the idea of dividing the country. The United States, too, had reinstalled collaborators into positions of power in the South, and had blocked an immediate withdrawal of foreign troops. Rhee's reliance on American backing only served to reinforce the widespread hostility toward his government.

When the North Koreans entered the South, the latter was on the verge of civil war. Uprisings and guerrilla activity against the Rhee regime took place deliberately to coincide with the crossing of the 38th parallel and, thus, to aid the communist takeover. Little resistance was offered to the advance, and few fled before it. As the North Koreans advanced, they installed Southern communists in positions of power, released political prisoners and enacted land reforms. It was with the introduction of U.S. ground troops into the country that this process came to a halt.

General MacArthur and his advisers had decided that it was necessary to build a defensive perimeter to halt the communists, and that they managed to do around the port of Pusan in the southeast of the country. While men and materials poured in through the port of Pusan throughout the summer of 1950, U.S. aircraft bombed and napalmed positions behind the enemy lines. By September 1950, a stalemate had been reached, with the communists controlling all but the southeast corner of the peninsula. As well as the monopoly of air space, MacArthur also now had more ground troops at his disposal than the Korean People's Army (KPA). He was therefore able to hold off repeated attempts to break through the defensive perimeter. But now the question was what next?

The South recaptured

The United Nations resolution had called for the repelling of aggression and the restoration of peace. That effectively meant that the KPA had to be pushed back to the 38th parallel. In working out how to achieve this, MacArthur confirmed his position as a leading military strategist. Against the initial advice of the Joint Chiefs of Staff in Washington, MacArthur ordered a seaborne invasion of Inchon on the west coast near Seoul, the capital of the Republic. The invasion coincided with a coordinated attack by United Nations troops to break out of the Pusan perimeter. The goal was to cut off supplies to the KPA and trap them within a pincer movement.

On September 15, U.N. forces landed at Inchon and the plan was put into effect, taking the communist forces completely by surprise. Within fourteen days, the United Nations troops had retaken practically the whole of the South. Seoul was recaptured on September 26, with the loss of 20,000 KPA lives and the near destruction of the city.

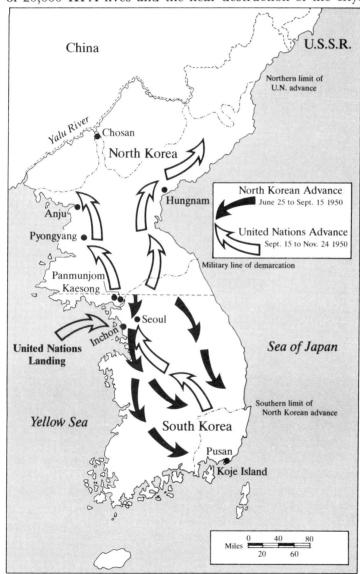

This map shows the course of events during the first few months of the war.

Tens of thousands of KPA troops and its supporters were
captured. The military strength of the North had been effectively wiped out. General MacArthur reinforced his status
as a war hero.

On September 28, Syngman Rhee, who had initially fled
to Pusan, was reinstalled as the head of government in Seoul.

At this stage, the original mandate of the U.N. had been fulfilled. The KPA was falling back in disarray to north of the 38th parallel, and the government of the Republic had been reinstated. In the U.S., the long-standing internal debate on the country's policy in situations such as that in Korea came to a head, and the war took a new turn.

U.S. Marines make the first landing at Inchon on the west coast, on September 15, 1950. Two weeks later, U.N. troops had retaken the South.

5
Containment or victory?

During the 1940s, the United States had developed a policy of containment in its response to the advances of communism in the world. Containment meant that the U.S. would not allow countries it considered strategically important to fall into the hands of communist regimes.

It was felt that in containing communism behind the "barrier" it had reached by the end of 1945, the U.S. would then be able to exert pressure on the Soviet bloc. That would eventually lead to the crumbling of Soviet influence in the world. That position was fiercely opposed by many members of the Republican Party in the United States, who

IN THIS ISSUE: TWO SIDES OF A GREAT DISPUTE

BY HARRY S. TRUMAN 'MacARTHUR LEFT ME NO CHOICE'

BY DOUGLAS MacARTHUR 'IT WAS A VENGEFUL REPRISAL'

TRUMAN AND MacARTHUR

Opposite
Syngman Rhee expresses his thanks to General MacArthur on the recapture of the capital, Seoul.

Left *This* Life *cover emphasizes the disagreement between President Truman and General MacArthur over Korean War policy.*

39

felt that the U.S. should show its strength and use its nuclear capability to win a decisive battle against the Soviet Union, before the latter developed nuclear weapons of its own.

The outbreak of the Korean War heightened the debate. President Truman and his Democrat supporters emphasized that the U.S. was limiting its objectives to containment and the reestablishment of the status quo in Korea—the division at the 38th parallel. Severe constraints were

U.N. troops crossing the Han River as the advance continued northward.

therefore put upon General MacArthur to avoid any military actions that would antagonize the Soviet Union or Communist China. MacArthur and the Republicans felt that those restraints were unrealistic. They wanted to unify Korea, and in order to win a decisive victory such actions might be necessary. They believed that the United States should be prepared to accept the consequences and risk an escalated war.

U.S. soldiers look out over the Yalu River, the border between Korea and China.

Reunification

With the near destruction of the KPA, the policy of limiting the war came under increasing strain. A new possibility presented itself: the reunification of Korea by force using U.N. troops. This possibility was positively advocated by Rhee. Entering the North entailed an increased risk of escalating the war, but the prize of reunifying the country was too great to resist. Therefore, a compromise was reached. The U.N. was to continue its advance northward, but was instructed to avoid military targets along the Yalu River

border with China, across which supplies flowed into the
North. MacArthur objected to the compromise, insisting
that he could not carry out the campaign under such restric-
tions, but he was overruled.

MacArthur was supported by Rhee in his objections. See-
ing the possibilities open to him, Rhee threatened to carry on
the advance without the support of the U.N. if necessary. On
September 27, the Joint Chiefs of Staff ordered MacArthur to
cross the 38th parallel and continue the advance as long as

there was a reasonable chance of success. Meanwhile, the United States used diplomatic channels to attempt to reassure China and the Soviet Union that the U.S. involvement in Korea presented no threat to them. The assurances implied containment, not the destruction of North Korea, but China and the Soviet Union remained unconvinced.

To maintain U.N. support, a new resolution had to be sought. On October 7, MacArthur appeared before the U.N. to give backing to the proposed reunification of Korea by force. A resolution was duly passed endorsing the action.

The first U.N. troops to enter Pyongyang, the North Korean capital, in October 1950.

In Korea, the war rapidly spread into the North. The remnants of the KPA and Kim Il Sung's government fell back toward the northern border with China. Success for the U.N. forces seemed assured. While one army unit swept up the western coast taking Pyongyang, the capital of the North, on October 19, a second unit landed on the east coast and began to advance toward the border.

It was only with the surprise attack by Chinese troops, 40 miles (65 km) south of the Yalu River on October 26, that the advance was halted and a new stage in the conflict began.

6
The Chinese intervene

In the initial stages of the Korean War, the Chinese had offered only moral support to the campaign being waged by the North. In 1949, Mao Zedong's communist regime had only just established effective control over mainland China. There were still areas of resistance to overcome, the most important of which was Taiwan. That had become the last haven for Chiang Kai-Shek's anticommunist Kuomintang (National People's Party). Taiwan was perceived to be a major threat by the new regime in Peking, as a possible

The Chinese nationalist leader, Chiang Kai-Shek.

Mao Zedong, leader of the Chinese communists, who, by 1949, had taken control of mainland China.

launchpad for a future invasion of the mainland by noncommunist forces and as an opportunity for the United States to support the Chinese nationalists.

It was therefore with some concern that the Chinese saw the Straits of Taiwan "neutralized" by the Americans in June 1950, as part of U.S. policy toward Korea. The introduction of the Seventh Fleet into the Straits effectively blocked any communist invasion of Taiwan. That action by the United States was taken as a precautionary measure against the threat of communism spreading throughout Asia. In exchange for that protection, Chiang offered to send 33,000 troops to Korea to support the United Nations action. MacArthur wished to accept this offer, but was vetoed by Truman who felt it would antagonize the Chinese communists. The Chinese communists viewed these events and the continued refusal by the United Nations to accept their delegate as the legitimate representative of the Chinese government with grave concern, and as a possible threat to their national integrity.

As the United Nations forces advanced toward the 38th parallel, the possibility that a reunified Korea, together with Taiwan, would be used as a springboard for U.S. intervention in mainland China became a major concern for the Chinese communists. Through diplomatic channels, Chinese officials let it be known that an invasion of North Korea would be seen to menace China's vital interests. As the threat of invasion increased, large numbers of Chinese troops were moved into the border area. Attempts by the United States to reassure the communist government of mainland China fell on disbelieving ears.

A woodcut showing Chinese People's Volunteers joining forces with the Korean People's Army.

China enters the conflict

Despite the U.N. policy of limiting the war to Korea, the Chinese had complained from early August 1950 of U.S. aircraft overflying their territory and bombing targets north of the Yalu River. As the U.S.-dominated U.N. troops moved nearer the border, the Chinese began to prepare for war. On October 14, feeling increasingly threatened, the Chinese began secretly sending troops disguised as volunteer soldiers into northern Korea.

The possibility of Chinese involvement had been discussed and dismissed by MacArthur and Truman. It was therefore with complete surprise that United Nations troops met resistance from Chinese forces at the end of October. Moving at night and staying well camouflaged by day, there was no prior warning of the presence of Chinese troops in the mountainous countryside. After initial engagements, the United Nations advance was halted and the Chinese troops disappeared back into the hills. For two weeks, from November 7 to November 26, there was very little military activity on both sides. Once they had established their presence, the Chinese fell back to await the response and build up the strength of their forces.

While diplomatic efforts were made by other United Nations members to engage China in discussions on the joint issues of Taiwan and Korea, MacArthur assessed the chances of achieving the goal of reunification. On November 24, unaware of the extent of the Chinese presence, he announced that the "end of the war" offensive would be completed by Christmas 1950. As the offensive began, the reorganized KPA and 300,000 Chinese troops counterattacked. With no apparent concern for their own losses, the communist forces began an onslaught against the superior firepower of the U.N. troops, which was to begin a rout and give them control of North Korea. Christmas did not see the end of the war, but a continuation.

The communists used the guerrilla tactics developed by Mao during the long war for control of the Chinese mainland. These tactics were totally unfamiliar to the United Nations troops. The Chinese use of large numbers of American weapons that had been captured from Chiang's army during their own civil war added to the consternation of the United Nations troops. In that confusing situation, it was not always possible for them to distinguish between friend and foe.

*Battle-weary North
Korean refugees
struggle south in an
attempt to escape the
continuous fighting.*

51

U.S. airmen standing by a bonfire of burning equipment as they await orders to leave Pyongyang during the U.N. retreat in the face of the advancing communist forces.

As they retreated, the U.N. troops put into effect a scorched-earth policy, destroying anything that might aid the enemy. Large numbers of refugees fled south in advance of the war, as Truman threatened the use of nuclear weapons; a threat disparaged by the Chinese, but frightening to many allies of the United States.

As they neared the 38th parallel, Zhou Enlai, the Chinese premier, put forward his country's policy on Korea. To secure communist control of the peninsula, reunification by

force would be attempted. On January 4, 1951, control of
Seoul once again changed hands, and complete victory for
the communists seemed imminent. However, at that stage,
the communist advance finally ran out of steam. At the same
time, the United Nations recognized that reunification was
not possible. The Korean countryside had been largely laid
to waste, and it seemed that the major powers were willing to
seek some compromise resolution to the conflict, but not
without further carnage.

7

Stalemate and negotiations

With the discovery of Chinese troops in Korea, the U.N. countries increased their supplies of soldiers and weapons in an attempt to halt the retreat. MacArthur and the increasingly strident Republicans renewed their argument for the

extension of the war to north of the Yalu River. However, with their allies expressing doubts about the wisdom of engaging in a full-scale war against China, the Americans reverted to their original policy of restoring the border between North and South Korea. MacArthur was critical of the decision, and his disapproval hindered the enactment of the policy. On April 11, 1951, he was relieved of his command and ordered back to the United States. Effectively, he had been fired.

MacArthur returned to a hero's welcome in the United States. On April 19, he addressed both Houses of Congress and defended the need to continue the war for a successful conclusion. Tickertape parades were held in his honor in

General MacArthur stands in an open car, showered with tickertape during a parade held to honor him on his return to the United States.

several major cities. The Republicans sought his support in attacking Truman's handling of the conflict. Reflecting the increased influence of Cold War attitudes in the United States at that time, it was argued that failure to engage the major communist countries militarily would weaken U.S. standing in the world. Right-wing Republicans attacked the Administration for being infiltrated by communists, claims that were never substantiated, although thousands of federal employees were fired. However, the Republican attitude hit a popular note with the American people—the war had brought the country many gains, but at the cost of many American lives.

The Truman Administration found itself in an impossible situation. The intervention of the Chinese meant a victory over the communists was out of the question. The only way to achieve the sought-after peace was through compromise. It became increasingly difficult to argue that the war could be won.

Communists retreat

MacArthur's replacement as Supreme Commander of U.N. forces was Lieutenant General Matthew Ridgway. On taking up his command, the heavily demoralized U.N. troops were straggled across a line roughly 62 miles (100 km) south of the 38th parallel. With a spring offensive expected by the communists at any time, it was decided to attempt to hold that line. When the offensive began on April 22, U.N. troops were ordered to inflict as many casualties as possible upon the communists, a process known as "the meatgrinder." Artillery, napalm and bombs inflicted massive numbers of casualties on the communist troops. The defensive line held and there began a slow war to push the communists back to the 38th parallel.

As well as the U.N. military tactics on the front, the communists faced other problems. The swift advance south had left their supply lines badly stretched. Road and rail links from the border to the front were continually bombed by U.S. aircraft. While these links were rebuilt, often overnight by the Northern population, the flow of supplies could not sustain the momentum of the early advances. Confronted by stiffening United Nations opposition, the communists were forced into a retreat.

During the spring of 1951, the U.N. forces pushed their opponents back to a line just north of the 38th parallel, at

Opposite
MacArthur's replacement, General Matthew Ridgway (on the right), arriving in Korea to take up his command.

57

which stage the advance was halted. A stalemate had been reached. Since neither side could unify the country, negotiations seemed appropriate. The U.S. had already established with the Soviet Union (whose advisers had appeared in North Korea earlier in the spring) that any talks would seek a military truce only. A political solution to Korea's problems would have to wait. As a result of growing pressure from U.S. allies, Ridgway was ordered to offer an armistice to the communists, which he duly did on June 29. On July 2, that offer was accepted by Kim Il Sung.

Preliminary talks to establish an agenda for the full armistice conference began at Kaesong, on the 38th parallel, on July 10. The Americans anticipated that a truce would be signed within six weeks. However, that was not to be the case. Another two years elapsed before a treaty was eventually signed. When the talks moved to Panmunjom on October 25, each side attempted to improve its military position in order to be able to negotiate from a position of strength. Massive defensive fortifications were built by both sides against the possibility of the negotiations breaking down. While the negotiators talked, the devastation continued, particularly in North Korea.

Opposite *U.N. planes bombard a communist-operated magnesium factory in North Korea. Bombing campaigns continued during peace negotiations.*

The arrival of the Chinese and North Korean delegates at the armistice conference in Kaesong.

8
An uneasy peace

U.N. troops evacuating a wounded man by helicopter. Both sides suffered heavy casualties.

Throughout the negotiations, each side attacked the other's stance. The U.N. negotiators continually accused the communists of stalling and delaying an end to the conflict. The communists accused the United Nations of making excessive demands upon them. Skirmishing continued along the front throughout the negotiations. The United Nations attempted to exert pressure on the communists by bombing

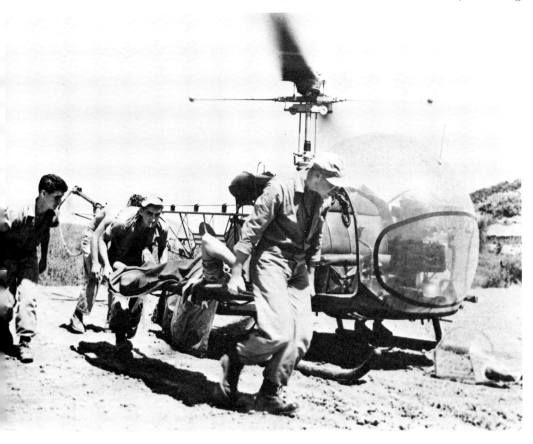

strategic targets in North Korea and north of the Yalu River. The communists attempted to gain international support for their position by accusing the Americans of using germ warfare against them. Although that charge was neither proved nor disproved, it caused great concern, particularly in Western Europe, where support for the war had come increasingly into question.

Two major issues prolonged the negotiations. The first was on precisely where the ceasefire line should be. The United Nations argued that it should be along the line of actual control. While that made military sense from the U.N.'s point of view, it meant that North Korea had to agree to the loss of some territory above the 38th parallel. Initially, the North Koreans refused to accept this. But, on October 31, they finally agreed to the United Nations proposal. However, the solution only increased the pressure upon the opposing armies to strengthen their military positions prior to signing any agreement.

Deadlock

An even bigger stumbling block to peace was the question of prisoners of war. Tens of thousands of Korean and Chinese troops had been captured during the course of the war. On Koje Island alone, near Pusan, there were in the region of

The end of the riot on Koje Island, where prisoners of war staged a violent protest against their extended imprisonment during the armistice negotiations.

165,000 prisoners. To begin with, the communists had wanted a ceasefire to precede the exchange of prisoners but, in January 1952, they conceded to the reverse proposal put forward by the United Nations. The main problem that arose from that agreement was whether prisoners should be forced to return to the countries they had fought for, or whether they should be given the choice of remaining in the country that held them prisoner. That issue of prisoners of war stalled the eventual signing of the armistice for eighteen months, adding a further 500,000 casualties to the war, most of them civilians.

The communists wanted the repatriation of all their prisoners. The U.N. would accept only voluntary repatriation. By May 7, the talks were deadlocked on this issue. In South Korea, communist prisoners of war staged riots and protests in an attempt to pressure the U.N. into resolving the issue. To coincide with the breakdown of talks, pro-communist prisoners on Koje Island seized the camp commandant to protest against their forced retention. Both sides attempted to gain a propaganda victory over the other in order to improve their negotiating position. In North Korea, U.S. Air Force prisoners were produced who publicly confessed to the use of germ warfare. Charges of brainwashing and maltreatment were also brought and caused bitter arguments.

While each side attempted to consolidate its hold over its respective territories against internal opposition, the U.N. developed various strategies designed to exert military pressure on the North in an attempt to break the deadlock at the talks. In the summer of 1952, Pyongyang suffered several major air strikes. In one raid on the city on August 29, American aircraft dropped about 700 tons of bombs and over 2,500 gallons of napalm. However, the communists refused to move from their position on the prisoner issue. It was only with the significant increase of military pressure following the election of the Republican candidate Dwight Eisenhower to the American presidency in November 1952 that the deadlock was finally to be broken, and voluntary repatriation was agreed.

Atomic threat

Korea was a central issue in the presidential election. The general dissatisfaction with Truman's policies was not improved by the deadlocked talks. Promising a swift end to

the war, Eisenhower won a landslide victory. He threatened to escalate the war against China and use atomic weapons unless the talks reached some conclusion. While facing increased opposition from Chinese planes based north of the Yalu River, the United States continued to escalate its bombing of North Korea. The decision taken in May 1953 to bomb major irrigation dams in the North was crucial to the breaking of the deadlock. It threatened the North's agricultural production, which was essential to sustain the communist war effort.

Coinciding with this increased pressure, an important change took place in the communist bloc with the death of Stalin in March 1953. Stalin had ensured Soviet support for the North Koreans during the war. Without Soviet backing,

U.N. troops block a demonstration by South Koreans during the armistice talks. The protestors were calling for reunification of their country.

China's entry into the war would not have been possible. The death of Stalin placed a question mark over future Soviet policy. At the same time, the failure to reunify Korea had led the Chinese to reassess their position. Their involvement in the war had been at great cost, at a time when they were seeking to consolidate their own control over mainland China. They did not want a protracted war against the United Nations forces.

General Mark Clark putting his signature to the armistice agreement that was finally signed on June 27, 1953.

Armistice reached

That combination of circumstances finally led to the communists accepting the voluntary repatriation of prisoners. On July 27, 1953, the armistice agreement was signed. The military conflict was effectively at an end. However, peace was far from secure. Syngman Rhee, who had re-established his government in Seoul, initially refused to accept the armistice agreement. He argued that it would result in the permanent division of the country and that without American support, the communists would once again attempt to overrun the South. He therefore threatened to continue the war on his own. To reassure him, the Americans offered a huge aid package to rebuild the economy of the South and strengthen its armed forces. They also decided that American troops would be left in position along the demilitarized zone between the North and South until a political solution to Korea's problems had been reached. Thus, a reluctant Rhee was eventually persuaded to accept the armistice. Without American support, he would have been powerless.

The conference to resolve the political questions over the

future of Korea met in Geneva in April 1954. Almost immediately it became deadlocked over whether foreign troops should be withdrawn prior to or after a political solution had been reached. The communists wanted immediate withdrawal. The United States wanted a political solution to come first. The dilemma that had arisen after the initial division of the country at the end of World War II was repeated.

The deadlock continues to this day. Korea is still divided by the ceasefire line, along which skirmishes take place. Although Chinese troops withdrew from the country in 1958, the demilitarized zone is guarded in the South by 40,000 American troops backed up with nuclear weapons. The armistice agreement brought the major military conflict to an end, but the peace it brought was an uneasy one.

A soldier of the Republic of Korea guards the barrier along the southern boundary of the demilitarized zone.

9
Korea, North and South

The war left Korea completely devastated. The cities of Seoul and Pyongyang were in ruins. The industries in the North had been completely destroyed by the bombing campaign. Huge numbers of refugees had left their homes in an attempt to escape the ebb and flow of the conflict. Economically and socially, the country was severely dislocated. Most important, it was still divided. The North had lost its traditional source of food, and the South had little in the way of modern industry. The regimes of Kim Il Sung and Syngman Rhee were left to rebuild their economies within the boundaries that had been set by the ceasefire agreement, while, at the same time, maintaining their commitment to Korean reunification.

In the North, Kim Il Sung consolidated his control of the communist regime while attempting to maintain the support of the different factions within the Korean Workers' Party. Following the death of Stalin, the Soviet Union began a policy of seeking peaceful coexistence with the United States, which earned the wrath of Mao Zedong. This eventually led to a schism between the two major communist powers in the late 1950s. In North Korea, which was heavily dependent upon aid from its neighbors, different factions supporting either China or the Soviet Union fought for control of the Party. In order to maximize the aid available for reconstruction, Kim Il Sung attempted to walk a tightrope between the opposing groups. Efforts were concentrated on rebuilding the industrial base of the country, which eventually gave North Korea a degree of self-sufficiency from its communist neighbors. That was displayed politically in the 1970s when North Korea joined the Non-Aligned Movement.

The cost of economic revival has been high. Wide-ranging reforms in the North to provide the population with basic welfare and educational services have been enacted at the

Opposite *The ruined shell of a North Korean factory after it was blasted with 248 tons of bombs by U.S. planes.*

expense of many social and political liberties. Kim Il Sung and his family are revered as cult figures, and are held personally responsible for all the major benefits that the North Koreans now enjoy. Although there is little doubting these impressive achievements, the responsibility for them lies firmly with the Northern population itself, who have rebuilt their war-ravaged part of the country with great determination and effort.

In the South, economic revival has also been the prime aim. That revival has largely depended upon attracting foreign investment. To achieve that, Rhee and his successors enacted savage labor laws designed to provide a cheap and mainly compliant work force. Over the years, the initial input of American aid has been largely supplanted by Japanese investment. The Korean War saw the beginning of the rehabilitation of Japan and was central to its economic revival following World War II. As the United States sought to reduce its direct involvement in Korea and turned its

Schoolchildren in present-day North Korea. Great advances have been made in education and other areas since the end of the war.

attention to the growing conflict in Vietnam, Japan was encouraged to increase its interests in the region. The economic revival in South Korea is due primarily to Japanese investment, which has caused a great deal of opposition within the country because of Korea's past history as a Japanese colony.

A series of increasingly authoritarian governments in South Korea have severely repressed opposition to their policies. All forms of opposition are regarded as being communist-inspired, which makes legitimate political activity against the government extremely difficult. Those in positions of power in the government have taken advantage of that situation for their own personal benefit. Despite attempts to eliminate corruption in the economic and political life of South Korea, it has remained endemic. The situation has proved to be a severe embarrassment to Western governments, who accept the Southern regime as the only legitimate government in Korea.

Although reunification is still a major goal for the North, it has become of less importance to the Southern regime, who associate it with communist control. The entrenched

Japanese investment in South Korean industry has paved the way for the country's present-day economic success.

positions of the two regimes, together with the global concerns of the United States, Soviet Union and China, have resulted in the peaceful reunification of the country becoming an increasingly distant prospect. The creation of a divided Korea at the end of World War II and all the ensuing problems effectively pushed aside the nationalist aspirations of the Korean people. As a result, two states have been created from one nation.

This South Korean patriotic poster reminds the people of June 25, 1950, the day the communists invaded.

Date chart

1910	Korea is annexed by Japan.
1945	
August 14	Japan surrenders at the end of World War II.
August 14	General Order No. 1 temporarily dividing Korea.
1948	
August 15	Establishment of the Republic of Korea in the South.
September 9	Proclamation of the Democratic People's Republic of Korea in the North.
1950	
June 25	Entry of Northern troops into the South.
June 27	U.N. passes resolution calling upon member states to repel aggression.
July 1	First U.S. troops arrive in Korea.
July 7	MacArthur placed in charge of U.N. forces.
September 15	Seaborne landing of U.N. troops at Inchon.
September 28	Rhee reinstalled as president in Seoul.
October 7	U.N. passes resolution calling for the reunification of Korea by force.
October 14	Chinese "volunteers" begin to enter Korea secretly.
October 26	First engagement between Chinese and U.N. troops.
November 24	Beginning of "end of the war" offensive by U.N. troops.
November 26	Counteroffensive by Chinese and KPA troops.
1951	
January 4	Seoul retaken by the communists.
April 11	MacArthur replaced by Ridgeway as commander of U.N. forces.
July 2	Armistice talks accepted by Kim Il Sung.
July 10	Armistice talks begin at Kaesong.
October 25	Armistice talks moved to Panmunjom.

1952

May 7 — Communist prisoners stage revolt on Koje Island.

November — Eisenhower becomes president of the United States.

1953

March — Stalin dies.

May — U.S. Air Force bombs major irrigation dams in the North.

July 27 — Armistice agreement signed.

1954

April — Geneva conference fails to reach a solution to the division of the country.

1958 — Withdrawal of Chinese troops from the North.

Glossary

Allied powers   The alliance of Britain, the United States and the Soviet Union during World War II, referred to as the "Big Three."

Annex   To add territory by occupation or conquest.

Armistice   A military truce.

Axis powers   The alliance of Japan, Italy and Germany during World War II.

Brainwashing   Exerting psychological pressure on people to change attitudes.

Capitalism   The economic system based on private enterprise in the free market and individual profit.

Casualties   In war, those killed, wounded, captured or missing.

Cold War   The state of political and military hostility between two countries falling short of actual conflict. This term is applied to the relations between the Soviet Union and the United States after World War II.

Communism   A classless society and economic system based on common ownership.

Containment   The policy of the United States toward restraining communism in the post World War II era.

Democrats   One of the two principal political parties in the United States. The other is the Republicans.

Engagement   In war, a battle or other military conflict.

KPA   The Korean People's Army (North Korea).

Kuomintang   Noncommunist Chinese Nationalist troops under the leadership of Chiang Kai-Shek.

Meatgrinder   The policy of inflicting maximum casualties, which was used by U.N. troops to halt the communist advance in Korea.

Napalm   A form of jellied gasoline that sticks and sets fire to anything it touches.

Nationalism   The desire for the self-government of a country by its people.

Non-aligned   A state or country that is not part of a major alliance or power bloc with countries such as the United States, Soviet Union or China.

Soviet bloc The countries under the influence of the Soviet Union.

Tribute A payment to a stronger country by a weaker country as a token of submission.

United Nations The forum of nations, established in the post World War II era, in an attempt to provide a peaceful means of resolving conflicts.

Volunteers The term given to Chinese troops fighting with the KPA.

Picture Acknowledgments

The publishers would like to thank the following for the loan of their photographs in this book: John Frost Historical Newspaper Service 8, 21, 39; Peter Newark's Western Americana frontispiece, 36, 60, 72; PHOTRI cover; Popperfoto 12, 15, 17, 18, 22, 26, 27, 29, 30, 31, 32, 33, 35, 38, 40, 42, 44, 47, 50, 52, 58, 59, 61, 63, 67, 71; Rex Features 70, 71; Topham 11, 23, 25, 46, 54, 56, 64, 65; Wayland Picture Library 14. The maps on pages 9, 24, 35 are by Malcolm Walker.

Index